DEAN

First published in Great Britain in 2019 by Dean,
an imprint of Egmont UK Limited
The Yellow Building, 1 Nicholas Road, London, W11 4AN
www.egmont.co.uk

Written and designed by Cloudking Creative

Copyright © Egmont UK Limited 2019

ISBN 978 1 4052 9783 7
70891/001
Printed in Italy

ONLINE SAFETY FOR YOUNGER FANS

Spending time online is great fun! Here are a few simple rules to help younger
fans stay safe and keep the internet a great place to spend time.
For more advice and guidance, please see pages 62-63 of this book.

- Never give out your real name – don't use it as your username.
- Never give out any of your personal details.
- Never tell anybody which school you go to or how old you are.
- Never tell anybody your password, except a parent or guardian.
- Be aware that you must be 13 or over to create an account on many sites. Always check
the site policy and ask a parent or guardian for permission before registering.
- Always tell a parent or guardian if something is worrying you.

Stay safe online. Any website addresses listed in this book are correct at the
time of going to print. However, Egmont is not responsible for content hosted by
third parties. Please be aware that online content can be subject to change and
websites can contain content that is unsuitable for children. We advise that
all children are supervised when using the internet.

Egmont takes its responsibility to the planet and its inhabitants very seriously.
We aim to use papers from well-managed forests run by responsible suppliers.

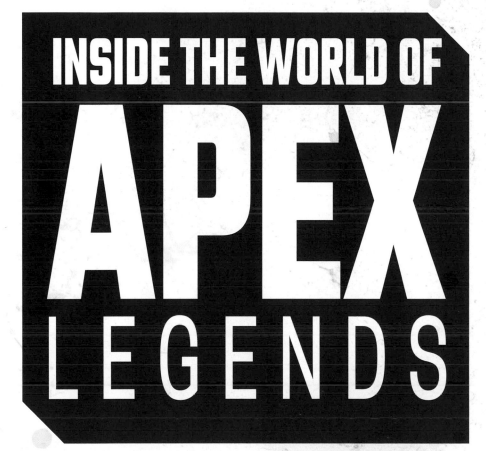

INSIDE THE WORLD OF
APEX
LEGENDS

CONTENTS

WHAT IS APEX LEGENDS?

Apex Legends is the latest in a line of hugely popular Battle Royale games. These are online-only multiplayer games with a twist – you have to be the last person standing. In each, a large group of people are dropped onto an island completely unarmed and forced to fight to the finish. A damaging and ever-shrinking circle pulls everyone towards one final battle. It makes for some of the most intense and incredibly addictive experiences you can have in a game!

Apex Legends has really changed things up. For one thing it features 60-player battles, not 100, which is the norm for games like *PlayerUnknown's Battlegrounds* or *Fortnite*. *Apex* is also a squads-only game, forcing you to team up in squads of three in order to take on 19 other squads.

THE STORY SO FAR...

The developers of the game, Respawn Entertainment, are the folks behind the hugely popular *Titanfall* series. Sadly there are no massive mechs in *Apex Legends* (yet!), but the story is set after the Frontier War players fought through in both games.

The War is over and worlds originally torn apart are now at peace. But at the fringes of the Frontier there are the Outlands, lawless worlds where only the crazy or violent once dwelled. Now that everything is much calmer, people take out their aggressions in the Apex Games, a new sport where Legends compete for money and for fame.

Good luck out there – you'll need it!

It's also a Hero Shooter. You don't pick a class here, you pick one of a number of unique Legends. Each Legend has exclusive abilities that completely change how you play the game and are made for different types of players. Some are better for lone wolfs, while others are made to support their squadmates. Some can call in a devastating aerial bombardment, while others have shields that protect you from incoming fire. You have to learn each Legend's abilities well, both so you know how to play as them and also so you know what to watch out for!

Plus, you've got to see how these folks move! The best part of *Apex Legends* may simply be how the game feels. Characters move fast, can slide down hills and climb up on top of buildings. The gunplay is satisfying and the sound design is perfect. Expect really fast, fun, and intense battles!

LAUNCHING AN INSTANT SUCCESS

As great as *Apex Legends* is, no one expected it to be the success it was. Being a free-to-play game helps, of course. But it's hard to pull people away from *Fortnite* – and *Apex* somehow managed to gain new players faster than *Fortnite* did!

QUIZ

HOW MANY PLAYERS DID APEX LEGENDS HAVE A MONTH AFTER LAUNCH?

100,000	10 Million
1 Million	50 Million

Answer: 50 Million

On release, EA Games enlisted some of the world's most popular streamers to switch games for a day and it paid off in a big way. *Apex Legends* quickly became the most-watched game on Twitch and stayed so for days, beating established juggernauts like *Fortnite* and *League of Legends*. This created a massive amount of buzz for a game that no one really knew was coming and it shattered viewing records. Soon everyone wanted to see what the big deal was about – this game looked fun!

Respawn says it didn't want to burn out the development team the way so many other studios had and instead focused on refining the core experience. They came back with a second season offering tons of new content and challenges – clearly listening to their fanbase. The future for the game is looking bright!

The first season showed how much potential the game had and how different it was from other Battle Royale games. The game's success even took Respawn Entertainment by surprise, and they frequently told people they were in this for the long haul.

DEFENSIVE CHARACTERS:

Pick a Defence Character when you want to battle tactically. The best way to play as one of these Legends is to plot your attacks and make your enemies come to you. Then spring your trap at the last second, surprising an entire squad if you're lucky. This means that you have to really be a team player!

Real Name:

ALEXANDER NOX

Age: 48
Homeworld: Earth

BACKSTORY

Caustic lives up to his name. A mad scientist who is only competing in the Apex Games in order to test out his deadly Nox gas, since there's no shortage of living specimens here.

ABILITIES

Passive Ability: *Nox Vision*
This lets Caustic see enemies moving through his Nox Gas.

Tactical Ability: *Nox Gas Trap*
Drops canisters that release Nox Gas when enemies come near. You can put down six at a time and surprise enemies coming through doors!

ULTIMATE ABILITY

Nox Gas Grenade
Spreads Nox Gas over a large area. Use this indoors, otherwise people can easily move away from the deadly fumes.

CAUSTIC

CHOOSE HIM

When you're feeling mean. Caustic is great for tricking people into his confusing and painful traps and he's downright evil in cramped indoor locations.

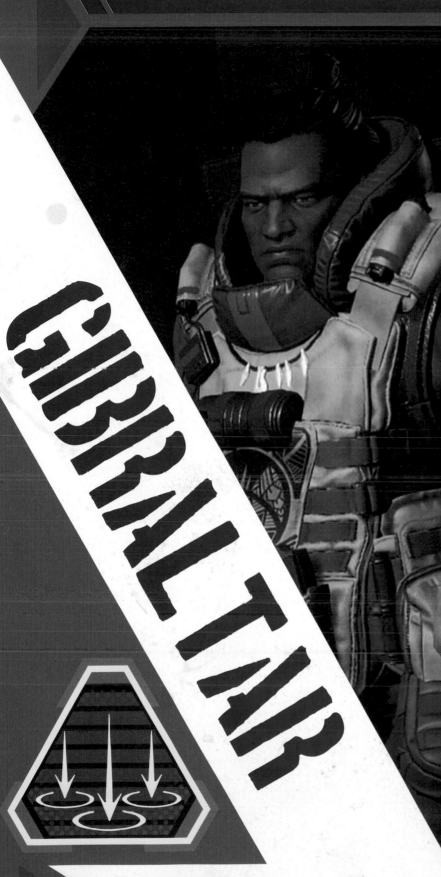

GIBRALTAR

CHOOSE HIM

When you're feeling protective.
He's super strong and menacing,
but he's a big teddy bear and
loves to support his
friends.

Real Name:
MAKOA
GIBRALTAR
Age: 30
Homeworld: Solace

BACKSTORY

Gibraltar was a rowdy kid until one day when he and his boyfriend stole his dad's motorcycle. They ended up getting trapped by a mudslide and saved by Gibraltar's parents, but his dad lost his arm in the process. Now Gibraltar has turned his life around and plays in the Apex Games to support his family, making sure to do everything he can to keep his teammates safe.

ABILITIES

Passive Ability: *Gun Shield*
The gun shield pops up when Gibraltar aims down his gun sights. This can be turned off if you like, but if you crouch and use this you'll be well protected all over.

Tactical Ability: *Dome of Protection*
Gibraltar throws out a dome shield that will block all attacks for 15 seconds – including your own! It stops bullets but it doesn't stop people from just walking in, so be careful an enemy doesn't just pop their head in and throw a grenade your way.

ULTIMATE ABILITY

Defensive Bombardment
Throws a marker that targets an area for bombing. A fierce and scary ultimate attack that can take down a whole squad.

DEFENSIVE CHARACTERS:

Real Name:
NATALIE PAQUETTE
Age: 22
Homeworld: Solace

BACKSTORY
The daughter of the Apex Games' lead electrical engineer. She shared the same interests as her father, who died just as his creation (the electrical Ring itself) was revealed to the world.

ABILITIES
Passive Ability: *Spark of Genius*
Ultimate Accelerants fully charge Wattson's Ultimate ability, even if she's at 0%. You'll no longer have to give every single Accelerant to Lifeline! Standing near Interception Pylons boosts the recharge of your Perimeter Security Tactical Ability.

Tactical Ability: *Perimeter Security*
Wattson will place nodes that can be connected to form electrical fences. Your squadmates will be able to travel through them, as they'll turn off for a second and allow them to pass, but enemies will take damage. Use this for defensive positions!

ULTIMATE ABILITY
Interception Pylon
Drops an electrified pylon that will not only repair everyone's shields within range, but it will shoot down any incoming ordnance.

WATTSON

CHOOSE HER
If you really like digging into an area and making your enemies come to you, then this is the perfect *Apex* character to select.

RECON CHARACTER:

If you want to play *Apex Legends* as a hunter, here's your best choice. Recon characters see the world differently to anyone else and can track enemies across all kinds of terrain. So far there's only one Recon character, but expect more to come soon!

BLOODHOUND

Real Name:
UNKNOWN
Age: Unknown
Homeworld: Unknown

BACKSTORY

Bloodhound is a complete mystery – no one even knows what gender they are. All anyone knows is that they are one of the greatest hunters ever seen. There are plenty of rumours about Bloodhound's real identity, of course. People whisper about them being a former slave, or a rich person getting their kicks, or a serial killer. Some of the crazier theories state they might be half-bat. Whatever the case, Bloodhound is a fierce opponent.

ABILITIES

Passive Ability: *Tracker*
Bloodhound sees icons that show where enemies walked and how long ago, allowing them to follow and take them out unawares.

Tactical Ability: *Eye of the Allfather*
Enemies and traps are briefly highlighted in red. This doesn't follow their movements, it just gives you an idea of nearby threat. Use it when you're suspicious you're being followed, or that someone is hiding in a nearby building waiting to ambush you.

ULTIMATE ABILITY

Beast of the Hunt
Bloodhound will move 25% faster. Their vision turns black and white, while enemies get highlighted in bright red. Use it to snipe far away enemies, or finish off one that you've been tracking.

CHOOSE THEM
If you like the idea of being the sneaky scout for your squad.

OFFENSIVE CHARACTERS:

Ready to run and gun? Choose one of these Legends. These are the characters leading the charge – the ones that like to shoot first and loot Death Boxes later. Not for the timid!

Real Name:
ANITA WILLIAMS

Age: 35
Homeworld: Solace

BACKSTORY

Even as a soldier from a family of soldiers, Bangalore stuck out. She graduated first in her class at IMC Military Academy, where she learned how to strip and assemble weapons blindfolded. During a recent mission Bangalore's team was ambushed and she lost her brother. Now she's trying to get back home to her remaining family, earning credits from the Apex Games to pay her way.

ABILITIES

Passive Ability: *Double Time*
When someone shoots at Bangalore she'll run 30% faster for two seconds. Use it to get her to cover.

Tactical Ability: *Smoke Launcher*
Fires a smoke canister from the launcher located over Bangalore's left shoulder. It blankets an area in smoke wherever it hits, letting her escape a battle or hide during an assault.

ULTIMATE ABILITY

Rolling Thunder
Bangalore calls in an artillery strike that drops rockets, which thud into the ground. After a few seconds they'll explode, doing 40 HP damage each. It's the perfect method to disperse enemies, allowing her to pick them off as they run around scared.

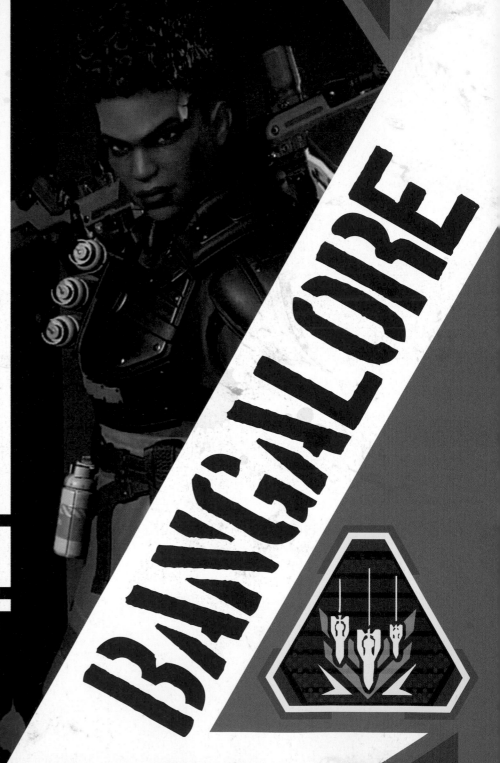

BANGALORE

CHOOSE HER

When you want to dive straight into a battle, leading your squad to victory.

OCTANE

Real Name:
OCTAVIO SILVA
Age: 24
Homeworld: Psamathe

BACKSTORY

Octane is a rich brat, the kind of kid that was given everything in the world and didn't appreciate any of it. His life bored him so much that he took up extreme sports, eventually joining the vicious Gauntlet. Determined to set a speed record on the course, he blew himself across the finish line with a grenade, which worked ... it just blew up his legs too. Oops. Thankfully he's good friends with Lifeline, who forged an order for new bionic legs, making him even faster than before.

ABILITIES

Passive Ability: *Swift Mend*
Can you say regeneration? You know you can. Octane is constantly getting health back.

Tactical Ability: *Stim*
Jabs an experimental medical stimulant (a 'Stim') into his arm that courses through his veins, making his movements 30% faster for six seconds. It costs 10% of his health to use, but Swift Mend means he'll be back to full in no time. While it's going back up he'll be zooming around the map, taking out oblivious enemies.

ULTIMATE ABILITY
Launch Pad
Octane throws out a jump pad that can catapults Legends through the air. He can use it to move into ambush positions on tops of buildings and ledges, or just to escape.

CHOOSE HIM

When you feel the need – the need for speed! Every other Legend will feel slow after stimming around the map as Octane.

Real Name:
ELLIOTT WITT
Age: 30
Homeworld: Solace

BACKSTORY

It turns out that Mirage has always been a class clown. Even though he was terrible in school he was great in his engineering classes and really loved playing with holo devices. He worked for years as a bartender and only joined the Apex Games after receiving his mother's blessing. Now he's determined to be a star.

ABILITIES

Passive Ability: *Encore!*
When Mirage is knocked down he'll automatically cloak and drop a decoy holograph, allowing him to crawl away somewhere safe if he's lucky.

Tactical Ability: *Psyche Out*
Sends a holographic decoy in whichever direction he chooses and highlights enemies that try to attack it. Those fools. Make sure that his decoy has open ground or it will hit a wall and stop moving; ruining the illusion.

ULTIMATE ABILITY

Vanishing Act
Deploys five decoys in a circle around Mirage, and cloaks him. Since enemies will know he's somewhere nearby, even if he's cloaked, this is maybe the most useless ability in the game! Stick to Psyche Out.

MIRAGE

CHOOSE HIM
When you definitely want to mess with people's heads. Psyche Out can be really, really fun.

Real Name:

REDACTED

Age: Redacted
Homeworld: Redacted

BACKSTORY

No one knows who Wraith is, not even Wraith herself. She woke up in a Detention Facility with no memory and then started hearing voices. It turns out that the voices were other versions of herself from alternate dimensions. They told her how to use the void to travel between them and awakened her abilities, allowing her to escape captivity. Now she's determined to find out who she is by breaking into research facilities hidden underneath the Apex Games.

ABILITIES

Passive Ability: *Voices from the Void*
A voice (a Wraith from another dimension!) warns her when danger is near. She can let her squadmates know about what she's seen with the press of a button.

Tactical Ability: *Into the Void*
Wraith shifts into void space, which makes her disappear from enemy view. She'll move fast and avoid damage, until the ability ends in three seconds. Perfect for escaping, or getting the drop on an enemy.

ULTIMATE ABILITY

Dimensional Rift
Wraith will open up a portal, move a short distance, and open up another one. These portals will remain linked for 60 seconds and anyone, on any squad, can use them. Want to quickly transport the team to a new location? This is the easiest way to do it. Or she can use them to set traps for curious enemies.

WRAITH

CHOOSE HER

When you're feeling sneaky and weird, or you just want to be by yourself – thousands of alternate versions of yourself!

SUPPORT CHARACTERS:

These Legends are just as good with weapons as the others, but their abilities are useful for helping out your squadmates. This makes them essential additions to any strong crew!

Real Name:

AJAY CHE

Age: 24
Homeworld: Psamathe

BACKSTORY

Lifeline left home after finding out that her family was making money from the war. She joined a humanitarian organization that helps communities in need, but they need money to operate. So she's joined the Apex Games in order to help fund it and help other people. It doesn't hurt that she's a brutal fighter and incredible combat medic!

ABILITIES

Passive Ability: *Combat Medic*
Lifeline uses healing and shield items 25% faster than anyone else, and can revive squadmates faster too. When she's reviving, a shield wall will generate in front of her to provide protection from any incoming gunfire.

Tactical Ability: *D.O.C. Heal Drone*
Lifeline's little buddy is the Drone of Compassion. When summoned the drone extends healing tubes that attach to a max of two nearby players and heals them.

ULTIMATE ABILITY

Care Package
Maybe the strongest Ultimate of any Legend, this calls in a drop pod from the sky. The pod contains three items, and can even hold Legendary weapons that can't be found anywhere else! Be warned – other squads will hear it coming and seek to take its goodies for themselves.

LIFELINE

CHOOSE HER

If you like the idea of being the healer on your squad, or being able to get the best gear on your own terms.

20

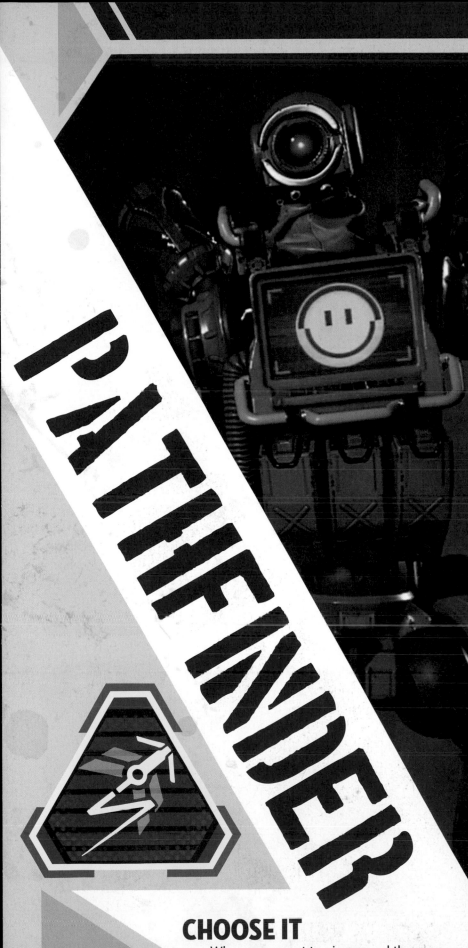

PATHFINDER

CHOOSE IT

When you want to zip around the map as quickly as you can and enjoy using the high ground.

Real Name:
MRVN
Age: Unknown
Homeworld: Unknown

BACKSTORY

Pathfinder is a MRVN (Mobile Robotic Versatile eNtity) that's been heavily modified for surveillance purposes. But it doesn't know why it was made. It booted up in an abandoned lab decades ago and has been seeking the reason for its creation ever since. In order to attract the attention of someone who might know it, it has decided to become a Legend in the Apex Games, and has proven itself an enthusiastic and vicious fighter.

ABILITIES

Passive Ability: *Insider Knowledge*
Allows Pathfinder to access survey beacons around the map. This reveals the Ring's next location, and gives your squad an edge on choosing where to relocate to.

Tactical Ability: *Grappling Hook*
Pathfinder throws a grappling hook that grabs onto objects and sends you hurtling towards it. It can also attach to players or ziplines! Use this to get on top or around objects quickly. The grapple doesn't just pull you in a straight line either, and can be used to swing around corners or up into the air.

ULTIMATE ABILITY

Zipline Gun
Pathfinder shoots out a zipline similar to the ones scattered all over the map. This new zipline will remain for the rest of the match and give you access to the top of structures, or simply provide an escape route for your friends when a Ring is closing in on you. You can even bait enemies into traps using it!

WEAPONS

Carried by most people, as they're useful in all kinds of battles. Their accuracy means that they're good for medium- to long-ranges and they do enough damage to be a standard weapon.

R-301 CARBINE

The R-301 is generally regarded as one of the best weapons in the game, which is surprising. It uses light rounds that don't do much damage, but it's fast and accurate and can even be fired from the hip effectively. Don't pass it up.

Pros
> Great range, rate of fire
> Doesn't have much of a kick

Cons
> Not as powerful as other ARs
> Low base ammo capacity

HAVOC

The Havoc was the first weapon added to the game and is still the only AR that uses energy ammo. Like other energy weapons it takes a second for the gun to spin-up and start firing, but it allows a number of attachments that make it more versatile than most. You can pick up either the Selectfire or Turbocharger hop-ups to either speed up the spin-up time of the rifle or enable a beam fire mode.

Pros
> High damage, good range
> Adaptable with hop-ups

Cons
> Has to charge up before firing
> You might die before it does

HEMLOK BURST AR

The Hemlok shoots a three-round burst and can cause an insane amount of damage if all rounds hit. It shoots them fast, too. If you'd rather slow things down and not have to reload as much, you can change to a single fire mode instead.

Pros
> High accuracy, insane damage in burst mode
> Good in medium-to-long-range battles

Cons
> Eats through ammo
> Slow between bursts, terrible at close-range

VK-47 FLATLINE

This is a solid weapon, but not if you are concerned about wasting bullets. It kicks like a mule and you'll have trouble keeping hold of it in full-auto mode, but if you get close enough to someone, you won't have to worry about accuracy.

Pros
> High damage (2x headshot damage!)
> Brutal at close-to-medium-range

Cons
> Terrible accuracy
> Poor at distance

SUBMACHINE GUNS

Fast and quick – these guns are perfect for close-range battles. Their bullet spreads mean that they're hard to control and terrible for long-range battles, but they can take an enemy out before they realise you're there.

ALTERNATOR SMG

The Alternator gets its name from its twin barrels, which alternate in order to speed up the gun's rate of fire. It's a small gun, almost pistol-sized and will eat up a magazine quickly. If you see it at the beginning of a match, you should grab it and if you happen to find the right attachments, it can do a decent amount of damage.

Pros
- Powerful if fully kitted
- Better than your fists

Cons
- Light damage
- Ploughs through bullets

PROWLER BURST PDW

Pros
- Great at close-quarters
- Insane DPS with Selectfire Receiver

Cons
- Burst-only without hop-up
- Devours bullets

This is the only SMG to offer a burst firing mode that blasts off a five-round shot. This makes it dangerous in the right hands, but also means you have to aim well and make them count. A 20-round magazine sounds hefty, but it means you only have four trigger-pulls before you'll have to reload, so keep track. Attach a Selectfire Receiver to turn it into a full-auto monstrosity.

R-99

A favourite of streamers everywhere. The R-99 does a ton of damage very quickly, even though it's very unassuming. It has a bit of recoil, but if you get a hold of this weapon it's one of the most dangerous ones around.

Pros
- High DPS
- Perfect for close- to medium-range

Cons
- Strong recoil pulls the barrel back
- Less effective at long-range

Light Machine Guns have huge magazines and do a ton of damage to enemies, although they take forever to reload and are hard to control. But with one of these you can take on anyone.

DEVOTION LMG

Pros
▷ Highest DPS of any gun
▷ Fierce when fully-kitted

Cons
▷ Energy ammo is harder to find and you'll need a lot
▷ Slow fire-rate makes you vulnerable during spin-up

Like the Havoc, the Devotion is an energy weapon. That means it takes a while to spin up and start firing, so don't look at your gun and think something's wrong when you pull the trigger and nothing happens for a second. When it finally starts firing anyone in your sights will soon wish they weren't. Plus, if you get the Turbocharger hop-up attached (which eliminates the spin-up time) you'll be almost unstoppable.

M600 SPITFIRE

Pros
▷ High damage, range
▷ Perfect against multiple opponents

Cons
▷ Slow reload
▷ Slower fire-rate than Devotion

If you absolutely, positively have to take out every last member of a squad, here's your weapon. It does a ton of damage and has so many bullets that you'll get more than enough chances at hitting your target. It also has surprisingly good accuracy for a weapon that spits out so many bullets. A favourite of many.

L-STAR

Pros
▷ High damage, fire-rate
▷ It's hard to hide from this one

Cons
▷ It eventually runs out of bullets
▷ When it runs out, it's useless

If you've played *Titanfall 2*, you've handled this gun. It's a full-auto gold weapon with so much force it can knock doors off their hinges. Given that it's so powerful it will only appear in air drops and you won't be able to get any more ammo than what it comes with, so make every shot really count.

PISTOLS

For the most part you'll probably skip over these during any serious match, but they have their uses. It's faster to switch to a pistol instead of reloading other weapons and in the beginning of a match they can mean the difference between life and death.

P2020

This is another weapon taken from *Titanfall 2*. It's a pretty standard semi-automatic pistol that shoots as fast as you can pull the trigger. It doesn't do much in the way of damage but it's still dangerous against an unarmoured opponent, or to finish off someone you've weakened with a better weapon.

Pros
- Good during the opening round
- Easily switched for a better weapon

Cons
- Not much damage
- It's a pistol

RE-45 AUTO

Pros
- Great rate of fire
- Quick reload time

Cons
- Huge amount of kick
- Will empty the magazine before you know it

This full-auto pistol can take out an enemy super quickly, but only if you can control its kick. It may be small, but this fast-firing weapon pushes you back into the air when you hold down the trigger. If you learn to tame it, you can do a ton of damage. Use it for the early game.

WINGMAN

While this gun has been nerfed a bit with its capacity, the Wingman still holds up as the best pistol in the game. It's the only one that takes heavy ammo and does so much damage that you'll only need a couple of shots to take someone out. Just don't pick it up if you're a terrible shot ...

Pros
- Insane damage
- Only pistol that can compete

Cons
- Only six round magazine capacity
- You need to know how to aim

SHOTGUNS

Just a couple of shots from one of these will take out most opponents and their spread of bullets ensures you just need to shoot near an enemy to do damage (of course, it doesn't hurt to get direct shots). They're essential for close-range battles.

EVA-8 AUTO

Pros
▷ Fastest firing rate of shotguns
▷ Can do an enormous amount of damage in no time

Cons
▷ Low damage per shot compared to other shotguns
▷ You'll run through lots of shells

This is an automatic shotgun that shoots faster than any other shotgun in the game. It doesn't do as much damage, but it just keeps firing. This is the kind of weapon that's so dangerous it can make a noob competitive.

MOZAMBIQUE

There's a reason your Legend will throw the Mozambique down in disgust when you switch to a better weapon – it's pathetic. It only carries three shells and barely does any damage. It's worth picking up if you can't find anything else at the start of a match, but you're better off with literally any other weapon in the entire game. Throw this away as soon as you can.

Pros
▷ It's a gun
▷ It makes a nice 'bang' sound

Cons
▷ It's a terrible, terrible gun
▷ Seriously, it's garbage

PEACEKEEPER

The favoured shotgun of enthusiasts everywhere. It does a massive amount of damage per shot and has surprisingly good range. It's good enough to compete without any attachments, although a Precision Choke hop-up will allow you to charge up your shots for even more precise aim. This is the shotgun to get.

Pros
▷ Massive damage
▷ Shoots 11 pellets in a tight star pattern

Cons
▷ Won't help you at long-range
▷ Won't contribute to world peace

MASTIFF

Okay, so we said the Peacekeeper is the shotgun to get, but the Mastiff is better in almost every way. It's also much more rare – it only comes from a supply drop. It also fires eight pellets with each shot in a wide spread, which can take almost any enemy down with a single shot. You won't find them often but when you do, use them.

Pros
▷ Does staggering 288 damage per shot
▷ Don't even need to aim

Cons
▷ Tiny four-round magazine
▷ Unique shotgun shells means only 20 shots

SNIPER RIFLES

Long-range fights are tricky in *Apex Legends* because a squad can easily retreat and patch up their wounds or pick up downed friends. But there's so many wide open areas that you'll need a gun with some reach or you'll get pinned down. These rifles will give you all the range you need.

G7 SCOUT

Pros
▷ Good damage, fire-rate
▷ Dangerous at close-, medium- and long-range

Cons
▷ Lowest DPS of sniper rifles

You can find the Scout just about everywhere, but unlike some other weapons (we're looking at you, Mozambique) it's well worth picking up. It does a decent amount of damage and it's effective at any range, even more so when you add Mag attachments to its already-hefty magazine. It's an extremely versatile weapon, maybe even the most versatile.

LONGBOW DMR

If you want to take an opponent out with one shot, this is your rifle. It does a lot of damage and is accurate across huge distances. Its slow fire-rate isn't too much of an issue if you learn how to land shots. If you're serious about sniper fire, practise with a Longbow.

Pros
▷ Great damage per shot
▷ Perfect for long-distance fighting

Cons
▷ Painfully slow
▷ Useless if enemy squads get too close

TRIPLE TAKE

Why shoot one bullet when you can shoot three? The Triple Take fires three bullets at once in a horizontal row, increasing the chances that you'll hit someone far away. But it also doesn't do as much damage as other sniper rifles, unless you manage to land all three shots.

Pros
▷ Lots of damage
▷ Energy bullets are faster than any other gun
▷ Great at mid-range

Cons
▷ Slow to reload
▷ Reliant on rare energy ammo

KRABER .50-CAL

This is another weapon with unique ammo that's only available through supply drops, and is just as powerful as you'd expect. Sure it's gigantic and clunky, but it can destroy an enemy with a single shot. It does a staggering 250 damage with a headshot, so work on aiming. If you can't aim it will get you killed as you struggle to load the next round.

Pros
▷ One shot, one kill
▷ Enemies won't know what hit them

Cons
▷ Takes forever to reload
▷ Only 4-round magazine, uses unique ammo

ITEMS | CONSUMABLES

These single-use items can be very powerful. Make sure to have at least a few ready. These can really increase your power! Grab too many, though, and you'll clutter your inventory.

ARC STAR

Does your enemy have a full Legendary shield? Not anymore, they don't! Throw an Arc Star and it will stick to any enemy or surface it hits, exploding and destroying any nearby shields completely. It will do 75HP damage and destroy doors as well!

[FULL] HOLD ○ SWAP   PING R1

Weapon | Thrown
ARC STAR

Sticks, then explodes after a short delay.
Causes damage and blurred vision.

FRAG GRENADE

If you've played any video games before, you know what frag grenades do (they go BOOM). They do a ton of damage depending on how close someone is to one when it goes off. You can even do trick shots with them, bouncing them around corners to take out unsuspecting enemies. Keep a couple on hand whenever you can. If you see a group of enemies and they don't see you, a volley of frag grenades from your squad will make them take notice.

THERMITE GRENADE

These grenades explode on impact, creating a wall of flames on the ground. If you get caught in the fire you'll take damage, but they're best used to trap people, or to prevent them from trying to revive their teammates. No one wants to jump into a fiery death trap.

Swap Grenade
R2 Throw Grenade
Tap Use Health Kit
Hold Use Ordnance Menu

ULTIMATE ACCELERANT

This item restores 20% of your character's Ultimate meter, allowing you to charge it up faster and take advantage of your Legend's unique abilities. Most people like to give it to Lifeline, since she has that incredible supply pod Ultimate. Wattson is another person who should hold on to a few, since her passive ability instantly fills her Ultimate meter with just one Accelerant!

Ultimate Accelerant
PRESS △ TO CANCEL

U-BATT
ULTIMATE ACCELERANT

ITEMS GEAR

You are useless without gear. You drop into the map with nothing but your fists, so you'll have to loot all you can in order to be prepared for the coming fight.

BACKPACKS

How are you going to carry all this loot? You're not wearing cargo pants! At the start of a match you only have eight inventory slots for all of the stuff you're going to pick up and it's not nearly enough. Backpacks offer new slots to fill up and can be found in four different rarities, including a super-rare Gold version.

Level 1 Common (White)	+2 Inventory Slots
Level 2 Rare (Blue)	+4 Inventory Slots
Level 3 Epic (Purple)	+6 Inventory Slots
Level 4 Legendary (Gold)	+6 Inventory Slots (Healing items take 50% less time to use)

Level 1 Common (White)	Absorbs 50 Damage
Level 2 Rare (Blue)	Absorbs 75 Damage
Level 3 Epic (Purple)	Absorbs 100 Damage
Level 4 Legendary (Gold)	Absorbs 100 Damage (performing Finishers fully regenerates shields)

BODY SHIELD

You can take 100 hit points (HP) damage before you're downed. Protecting your life with a body shield is important! Shields give you extra protection in a battle, as any shots you take will chip away at your shield before affecting your HP. They come in four different rarities that offer increasing protection.

HELMET

Shields protect your body, but headshots are super dangerous. Stick a helmet on your head and you'll help eliminate any headshot bonus that a sniper is aiming for. They come in four different rarities.

Level 1 Common (White)	Reduces headshot bonus damage by 30%
Level 2 Rare (Blue)	Reduces headshot bonus damage by 40%
Level 3 Epic (Purple)	Reduces headshot bonus damage by 50%
Level 4 Legendary (Gold)	Reduces headshot bonus damage by 50% (Reduces Tactical and Ultimate recharge time)

KNOCKDOWN SHIELD

Getting knocked down is one of the most frustrating moments in the game, but knockdown shields allow you to protect yourself a little more. Enemies will seek to eliminate you completely, but you can prevent this by raising your knockdown shield and giving your friends time to come and save you. As with the other items, knockdown shields come in four different rarities:

Level 1 Common (White)	Provides protection against 100 damage
Level 2 Rare (Blue)	Provides protection against 250 damage
Level 3 Epic (Purple)	Provides protection against 750 damage
Level 4 Legendary (Gold)	Provides protection against 750 damage (can self-resurrect once after being knocked down)

ITEMS SHIELDS

If you want to stay in the battle, you're going to want to keep your body shield full at all times. Note that the Death Boxes enemies leave behind sometimes hold their body shields and switching to a new one of the same type is a lot easier and faster than recharging it with a shield cell or battery.

SHIELD BATTERY

These take five seconds to use but fully recharge your shields, no matter what rarity of shield you have. You can store three in every inventory slot and you'll probably need them all if you get to the end-game.

SHIELD CELL

These items restore a single bar of your shields. They work in a mere three seconds, but if you have a rare or Epic shield it's going to take a few of them to get you up to full strength.

PHOENIX KIT

Escaped a battle with no shields and your health all the way down? Phoenix Kits will bring you back from the dead. They don't stack in your inventory, meaning you can only carry one per slot. They also take a full ten seconds to work. Even being as slow as they are, they can be incredible for later stages of a round, as they can bring you back to fighting form in one shot, rather than making you fiddle with both healing and recharging items.

PICK UP   PING R1

PHOENIX KIT
Heals 100 health and 100 shields.
10 second use time.

HEALING

Just like your shields, you're going to want to keep your health at max. You only have 100 hit points (HP) and as you get damaged it reduces until you're knocked down. Heal yourself every chance you get – sometimes even during a lull in a firefight! Keep healing items on hand, unless you're Octane (whose passive ability lets him regenerate) or have Lifeline on your team (she can heal people with her tactical ability). That's the only way to ensure you'll stay in top fighting form.

MED KIT

These will fill your health completely, but they'll take eight seconds to do it. This is the item to use when your health is dangerously low. You can fit two in a slot, so grab them if you ever find them.

Mirage: Got a Hop-Up here.

PICK UP   PING
MED KIT
Heals 100 health.
8 second use time.

SYRINGE

Syringes work faster than med kits – they only take five seconds – but they heal 25 HP. They're much more common than med kits though and allow you to heal no matter the situation.

MEDIX

PICK UP   PING
SYRINGE x2
Heals 25 health.
5 second use time.

ITEMS ATTACHMENTS

Attachments can make the lousiest weapon into a force to be reckoned with (unless that weapon is a Mozambique, naturally). They can be found all over the world, and are equipped automatically when you pick them up. Other games make you fuss around in the menus, but *Apex Legends* wants you to keep playing!

All the items in *Apex Legends* come in a variety of different colours that show how good they are.

White	Rare	Purple	Gold
Common	Blue	Epic	Legendary

That makes it easy to see what's the best and what you should try and grab. It's simple to remember – always go for the gold.

MAGAZINES

Every weapon comes with a standard magazine that fits a number of bullets, but by equipping an extended magazine you can increase that amount. More bullets per magazine means more shots before you have to reload, which can make all the difference in a match. They come in all four varieties, and at rare (blue) levels and above the light and heavy mags also reduce reload time.

EXTENDED LIGHT MAG
All light ammo weapons

EXTENDED HEAVY MAG
All heavy ammo weapons

SHOTGUN BOLT
Shotguns

WEAPON STOCKS

Stocks let you draw your weapons faster and also help them from kicking so much while firing. You can find them in the usual four varieties, from Common to Legendary. They're essential if you're using a weapon that fires bullets all over the place, like an LMG or SMG.

STANDARD STOCK
Weapons: LMG, SMG, AR

SNIPER STOCK
Weapons: Sniper Rifle

BARREL STABILIZERS

These attachments reduce the amount of recoil, or kick, that a weapon gives. They're great for fully automatic weapons, because those guns are hard to hold onto when they start firing! Attaching a stabilizer means that they're easier to control.

They come in Common, Rare, Epic and Legendary versions. The Legendary rarity has a bonus ability that reduces muzzle flash, making it harder for your enemies to see the position you're firing from.

HOP-UPS

Hop-ups can change a weapon completely. They're very rare, so if you see one that you can't use, make sure to notify your team where it is using the ping system. There are many different kinds but each one only fits a couple of different types of weapon.

PRECISION CHOKE
Allows you to hold down the fire button to charge up a tighter spread
Weapons: *Peacekeeper, Triple Take*

SELECTFIRE RECEIVER
Enables full-auto firing mode
Weapons: *Prowler, Havoc*

SKULLPIERCER RIFLING
Increases headshot damage
Weapons: *Longbow, Wingman*

TURBOCHARGER
Reduces spin-up time for energy weapons
Weapons: *Devotion, Havoc*

OPTICS

If you want to be able to hit someone who's not right in front of you, you'll need optics. You can find optic sights for every single kind of engagement and your weapon should always have one. Close range battles can be aided by 1x or 2x sights. Sniper rifles get higher numbers of course, all the way up to 10x so that you can headshot enemies all the way across the map.

VARIABLE SIGHTS
Some optics offer two different zooms in one. Use the smaller numbered zoom to get a look at the whole map before switching to the stronger zoom to pinpoint your enemies.

THREAT HIGHLIGHTING
These optics highlight your enemies in red, all the better to shoot them. It will even light them up through smoke or gas.

CLOSE-RANGE SIGHTS

1x Holo	Common (White)	All weapons
1x Digital Threat	Legendary (Gold)	Shotgun, SMG, Pistol - Threat Detection
1x-2x Variable Holo	Rare (Blue)	All weapons, Variable Sight
1x HCOG 'Classic'	Common (White)	All weapons
2x HCOG 'Bruiser'	Rare (Blue)	All weapons

MID-RANGE SIGHTS

3x HCOG 'Ranger'	Epic (Purple)	AR, LMG, Sniper, SMG
2x-4x Variable ACOG	Epic (Purple)	AR, LMG, SMG, Sniper, Variable Sight 1x-2x

LONG-RANGE SIGHTS

6x Sniper	Epic (Purple)	Sniper
4x-8x Variable Sniper	Epic (Purple)	Sniper, Variable Sight
4x-10x Digital Sniper Threat	Legendary (Gold)	Sniper, Variable Sight, Threat Detection

PICKING THE PERFECT CHARACTER

This quiz will help you choose the perfect character! Write down your answers to all the questions and tally up which ones you pick.

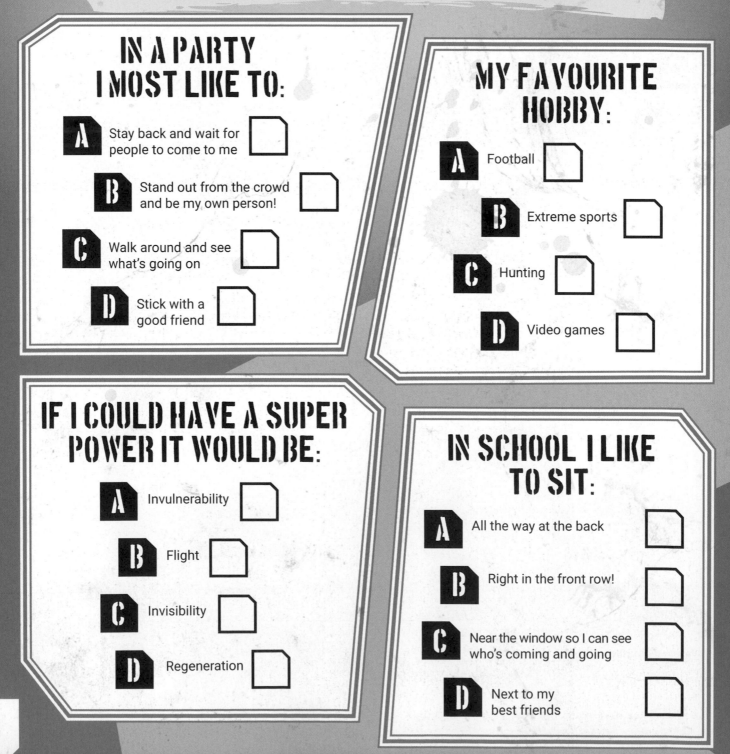

IN A PARTY I MOST LIKE TO:

A Stay back and wait for people to come to me ☐

B Stand out from the crowd and be my own person! ☐

C Walk around and see what's going on ☐

D Stick with a good friend ☐

MY FAVOURITE HOBBY:

A Football ☐

B Extreme sports ☐

C Hunting ☐

D Video games ☐

IF I COULD HAVE A SUPER POWER IT WOULD BE:

A Invulnerability ☐

B Flight ☐

C Invisibility ☐

D Regeneration ☐

IN SCHOOL I LIKE TO SIT:

A All the way at the back ☐

B Right in the front row! ☐

C Near the window so I can see who's coming and going ☐

D Next to my best friends ☐

AMONG MY FRIENDS I'M MOST KNOWN FOR:

A Being protective of them ☐

B Being the leader of the group ☐

C They barely know I'm there ☐

D Always being there for them ☐

MY DREAM PET:

A Turtle ☐

B Cat ☐

C Falcon ☐

D Dog ☐

MY IDEAL DAY WOULD BE:

A Staying at home! ☐

B Visiting new places ☐

C Going on a hike ☐

D Partying with friends ☐

WHAT TYPE OF LEGEND ARE YOU?

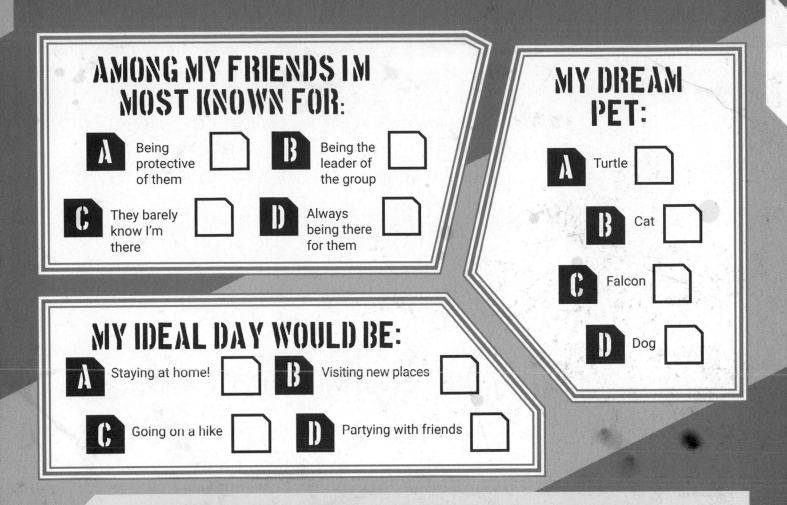

MOSTLY A

DEFENSIVE

You'll like having abilities that determine when and where the battle happens, on your own terms. Let the others run off and be fools – you'll be waiting for them.

MOSTLY B

OFFENSIVE

You don't like waiting around for things to happen, you want to make them happen yourself. If you see an enemy you will pursue them until they are totally destroyed!

MOSTLY C

RECON

You can see things others can't. You like to hide in the shadows and make sure people underestimate you, until it's too late for them.

MOSTLY D

SUPPORT

You know that a team is only strong when you're helping others to be their best. You will give them everything they need to achieve that. By sticking together, you will win!

JUMPING IN AND LOOTING

Once you've teamed up with two other players and picked your Legend, it's time to jump.

Just like in *Fortnite* and *PUBG*, you start in a dropship that flies across the map in a random direction. If you chose your character last, you're the Jumpmaster. It's up to you to choose when and where your squad jumps and where you land. On the map you can see a bunch of named locations, but you never know which ones will have the best loot. You also never know where other squads are going to go – and where you might end up immediately in a firefight!

So being Jumpmaster is a lot of responsibility to be sure! If it's too much, you can just pass it on to a squad mate.

Look around before you jump! In each match there will be some hints of popular areas that you can immediately head to, or avoid, depending on how you're feeling.

SUPPLY DROPS

Once in a while you'll see a rocket streaking down to earth. That's a Supply Drop, a giant metal pod that contains three handy items for anyone lucky enough to get there on time. Supply Drops are your only chance to grab a few of the rare Legendary items, some that can eliminate players with a single shot! But of course a rocket makes a lot of noise and everyone will see it … making it a prime target, and a place where battles are almost guaranteed.

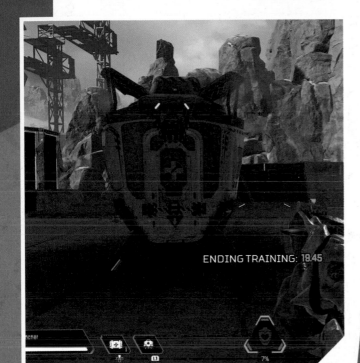

HOT ZONE

See that blue circle? That means that location has high-tier loot, which is the only place that will possibly have Legendary weapons – fully kitted weapons that can't be improved any further. This makes the Hot Zone a really popular place and makes for some guaranteed battles at the start of the game. This was such a good idea that *Fortnite* was quick to borrow it!

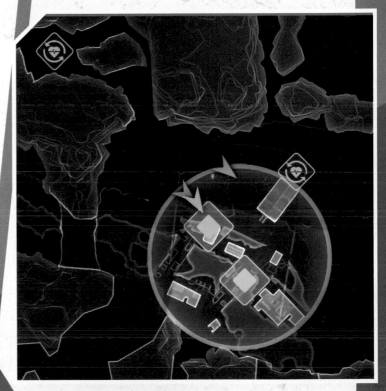

SUPPLY SHIPS

This ship is guaranteed to be filled with sweet, sweet loot. It's also guaranteed to draw lots of squads interested in taking all that loot. Sometimes heading straight to it can mean your team gets well-equipped right from the start, putting you in a great position to win the match. Sometimes you'll get there a second after another squad has picked up the weapons and will immediately die. It's a gamble.

If you do jump to the supply ship, just be careful to aim at it and don't undershoot. There's nothing more embarrassing than slamming into the side of it and falling to the ground!

PLAYING AS A TEAM

Apex Legends is a squads-only game, at least currently. Everyone plays on teams of three players and that means you really have to work as a team. While you can drop solo, it's almost never a good idea to do so. Stick together!

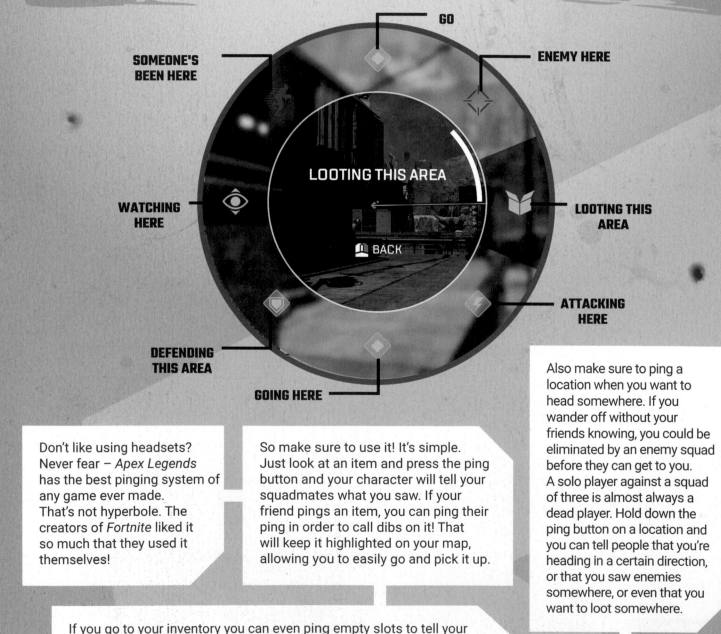

GO

SOMEONE'S BEEN HERE

ENEMY HERE

WATCHING HERE

LOOTING THIS AREA

BACK

LOOTING THIS AREA

ATTACKING HERE

DEFENDING THIS AREA

GOING HERE

Don't like using headsets? Never fear – *Apex Legends* has the best pinging system of any game ever made. That's not hyperbole. The creators of *Fortnite* liked it so much that they used it themselves!

So make sure to use it! It's simple. Just look at an item and press the ping button and your character will tell your squadmates what you saw. If your friend pings an item, you can ping their ping in order to call dibs on it! That will keep it highlighted on your map, allowing you to easily go and pick it up.

Also make sure to ping a location when you want to head somewhere. If you wander off without your friends knowing, you could be eliminated by an enemy squad before they can get to you. A solo player against a squad of three is almost always a dead player. Hold down the ping button on a location and you can tell people that you're heading in a certain direction, or that you saw enemies somewhere, or even that you want to loot somewhere.

If you go to your inventory you can even ping empty slots to tell your squad what you need, so that they'll look for it and ping you when they find it.

>> TEAM QUIZ <<

In *Apex Legends* you live or die by your team. To truly succeed you're going to have to look out for your squad and keep everyone alive. Take this quiz to see and then check your answers at the bottom of the page to see how well you've done!

WHEN YOUR SQUAD COMES ACROSS ANOTHER FULL SQUAD DO YOU...?

A Pick a single enemy each to fight.

B Concentrate your fire on one target and pick them off one by one.

C Run away – you're a pacifist!

THE REST OF YOUR TEAM JUST GOT ELIMINATED BY AN ENEMY SQUAD THAT'S LOOTING THEIR BOXES. DO YOU...?

A Run and don't stop.

B Hang back and wait for them to leave so you can retrieve them.

C Attack immediately – you can't take my friends' stuff!

YOU SEE A BUILDING THAT HASN'T BEEN LOOTED YET WHICH IS A DISTANCE AWAY FROM YOUR TEA§M. DO YOU...?

A Ping it and let your squad know you want to check it out.

B Head over immediately so you can get the best loot.

C Ignore it. Who really needs loot, anyway?

A SNIPER BULLET JUST STREAKED BY YOUR HEAD. WHAT DO YOU DO...?

A Stand still and look around for the sniper.

B Don't worry about it, they're probably far off.

C Run to cover and let your squadmates know what happened while constantly moving.

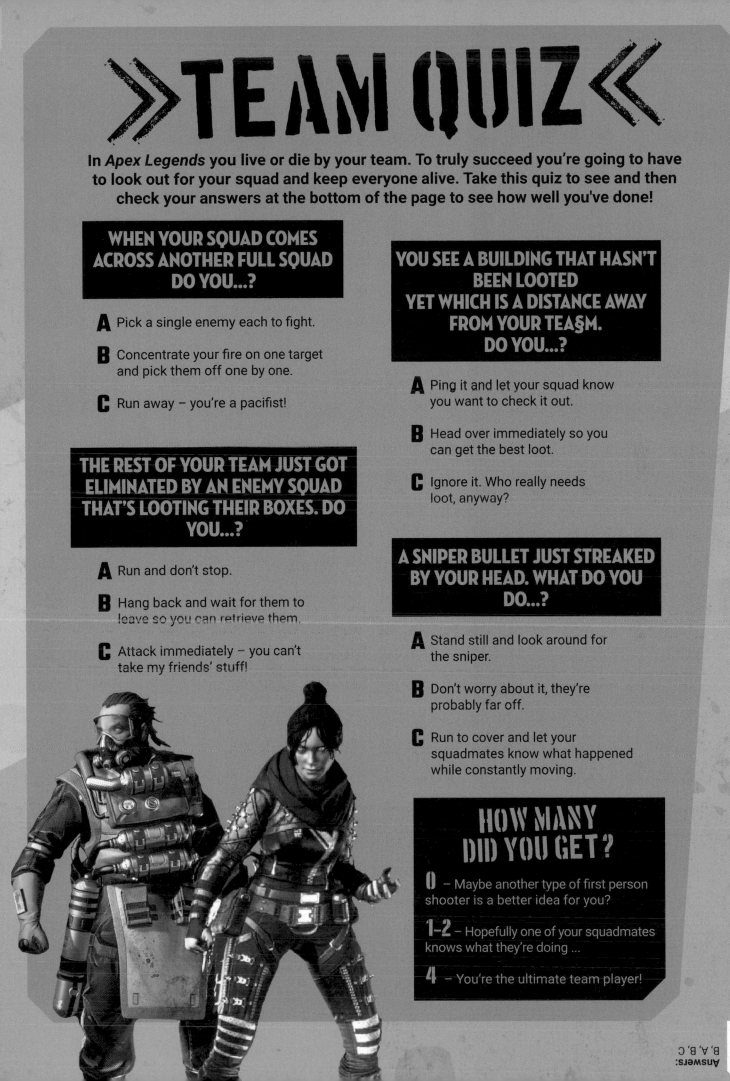

HOW MANY DID YOU GET?

0 – Maybe another type of first person shooter is a better idea for you?

1-2 – Hopefully one of your squadmates knows what they're doing ...

4 – You're the ultimate team player!

REVIVING AND RESPAWNING

In most Battle Royale games, if your health hits zero, you're dead and out of the match. Not so in *Apex Legends*! Even when you're dead you still have a chance to get back in the game. There are a few states you need to know …

KNOCKED DOWN

When your HP hits zero, you'll fall to your knees. You're completely defenceless at this point and can't use any weapons. If you have a knockdown shield you can raise it to stop enemies from shooting you, but you're a sitting duck. Even if someone doesn't shoot or execute you, you only have a limited time before you completely bleed out.

REVIVING

When you're knocked down, another player can pick you back up and get you back in the game. If they are attacked while holding the button to revive you they'll stop, so it's important to only start reviving once you're out of danger. Otherwise you'll just make an easy target for another squad. Characters like Gibraltar can protect you with a defensive shield, while Lifeline is faster at reviving than anyone else.

ELIMINATED

When you die from being knocked down, you're eliminated. But don't disconnect from the match yet! Your friends can still save you. When you die you leave behind a Player Banner in your Death Box alongside all your loot. If your friend picks that up they can bring it to a respawn beacon and get you back in the game!

» MOST KILLS «
TWITCH STREAMER MENDOKUSAIIX GOT 36 KILLS IN A SINGLE MATCH – CAN YOU BEAT THAT?

AWAITING RECOVERY

87.7

RESPAWNING

After a squad member brings your banner back to a respawn beacon, you'll fly in on a brand new supply ship, good as new. And we mean new. You won't have anything on you, just as if you had started the match over again. If you're lucky you can get back to your Death Box and reclaim your stuff, but you might need to find some new weapons and equipment if it's been looted.

Welcome to the Apex Games. Kings Canyon is the first and only map that *Apex Legends* has, so you'll need to learn its many varied locations. It's got rivers, deserts, military bases and giant monster bones littered throughout. Explore it well.

LEARNING THE TERRAIN

Kings Canyon is much bigger than it looks and it takes a while to travel across it. There are some handy ways to speed up your trek, though!

ZIPLINES

The wires strung up all around the map are actually ziplines. By grabbing one you'll go flying to the end of the line, allowing you to zoom across the map. They're great to get on top of structures and to move fast when the Ring is closing in on you. You can even shoot while holding onto a zipline!

JUMP TOWERS

See that red balloon floating in the sky? No, it's not from a party – that's a way to get around the map super-fast. The wire the balloon is connected to is actually a zipline that you can grab for a one-way trip straight up. When you hit the top you'll shoot out in a glide like it was the beginning of the match again. This lets you fly far across the terrain, essential when you're stuck near a closing ring.

WHO DID IT FIRST?

Apex Legends may have followed in *Fortnite*'s path, but it sure stole a little of the giant's spotlight when it hit. It had many new features that were attractive to Epic Games, so much so, that they immediately took inspiration from them! But who did what first?

PING SYSTEM

APEX LEGENDS ☐
FORTNITE ☐

BATTLE PASS

APEX LEGENDS ☐
FORTNITE ☐

RESPAWN BEACON/ RESPAWN VANS

APEX LEGENDS ☐   FORTNITE ☐

REVIVING

APEX LEGENDS ☐   FORTNITE ☐

SEASONS

APEX LEGENDS ☐   FORTNITE ☐

BATTLE ROYALE

APEX LEGENDS ☐
FORTNITE ☐

SUPPLY SHIPS

APEX LEGENDS ☐
FORTNITE ☐

CHALLENGES

APEX LEGENDS ☐   FORTNITE ☐

HERO SYSTEM

APEX LEGENDS ☐
FORTNITE ☐

DAILY/WEEKLY CHALLENGES

APEX LEGENDS ☐   FORTNITE ☐

LIMITED TIME MODES

APEX LEGENDS ☐
FORTNITE ☐

HOT ZONES

APEX LEGENDS ☐
FORTNITE ☐

JUMP TOWERS/ SLIPSTREAMS

APEX LEGENDS ☐   FORTNITE ☐

Answers: Ping System (AL), Battle Pass (F), Respawn Beacon/Respawn Vans (F), Reviving (AL), Battle Royale (F), Seasons (AL), Supply Ships (AL), Challenges (F), Hero System (AL), Daily/Weekly Challenges (F), Jump Towers/Slipstreams (AL), Hot Zones (AL), Limited Time Modes (F).

ALL THE LOCATIONS

HIGH-TIER LOCATIONS

These places are most likely to have the best loot, but it's not guaranteed! The tier changes every single match, so you might end up not finding anything that great, but these locations are your best bet.

ARTILLERY

This is a military base, so you know they left some good loot behind. This is a huge area with two hangars, lots of buildings and so much loot.

AIRBASE

This is where the dropships hang out in their free time. There are two landing strips over a cliff, one that's easy to fall into if you're not careful. This is a popular area and you'll have to worry about close- and long-range engagements from the other landing strip. Tons of supply boxes can be found here though!

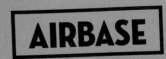

BUNKER

This is a narrow corridor that was dug through a mountain. If you want to get into a close-quarters battle, you should head right to Bunker. People love flying straight into the Bunker with Caustic and Wattson on their squad, just so they can really utilise their traps indoors. Plus, there are usually some great weapons and equipment to be found.

RELAY

A bunch of giant radar dishes make this location easy to see from the dropship, but it's usually far from the action. It can be a great starting point for your match, though, since it usually has so much sweet sweet loot. Just be careful not to fall into the river!

REPULSOR

Another military base like Artillery, again one that seems like the military just left all their best equipment behind. Take note of the underground tunnel that runs underneath – it can save you in a pinch, or even be used for ambushes.

ALL THE LOCATIONS

HIGH-TIER LOCATIONS

RUNOFF

It's everyone's favourite place – the sewage treatment plant. You might want to keep out of this water, though. Stick to the buildings, which can have all kinds of great things to pick up. Just be ready to hold your nose!

SWAMPS

We're not sure who was living on these little houses on stilts in the swamp, but they left behind all kinds of goodies. Stick to high ground and stay out of the water, as it will give you an advantage.

THE PIT

This area is tiny, but has a bunch of supply bins and chances for loot. Just try not to get stuck in it – there are only three narrow paths leading to it, making it a good choke point for anyone not looking out.

THUNDERDOME

It's clear that this area used to feature some kind of brutal fights, possibly involving the local animals. There are giant cages connected by ziplines and, as always, you should aim for the high ground if you get in a fight here.

WATER TREATMENT

Another good starting point for a match, as it's located at the edge of the map. Ignore the water treatment vats, which are empty! Open all the supply bins, grab all the loot from the buildings, and fly off to your next location from the jump tower.

ALL THE LOCATIONS

MID-TIER LOCATIONS

These have a good chance of being stocked with loot, but it can be more of a gamble. Aim for these locations as the ring closes.

BRIDGES

This is a wide-open location with lots of different levels, making it a good spot for snipers. But the couple of bridges and handful of structures don't give people much of a reason to hang out here. You'll have to be quick to take someone out here as they're most likely just passing through.

CASCADES

This location doesn't look like much, but it can be popular. The watchtower at the north can house some great loot and it overlooks the river underneath, providing good sniper opportunities. The only issue is that there are lots of places people could fire on you from, so stay alert!

SLUM LAKES

If, for some reason, you want to find out where the sewage from Runoff goes, head to the Slum Lakes. Whoever used to live here probably had to put up with a real stink, but there are many varied structures to loot here, giving you a good opportunity to stock up.

SKULL TOWN

This location was rated the most popular in the game in a recent Respawn Entertainment poll, so this isn't the place to go if you're hoping to avoid combat. You can almost guarantee to have a number of squads jumping right to it, mostly because it has dozens of buildings all filled with loot.

WETLANDS

Another small location you'll usually loot while heading to better locations. It's surrounded by empty land, making it either a good spot to engage incoming players, or a place to get trapped by multiple squads.

OTHERS

These are the weakest areas. They'll still have loot, sure, but their giant open spaces and potential traps make them less appealing.

HYDRO DAM

This concrete area looks like it will have a ton of loot, but almost always disappoints. It's an awkward place for firefights too. A good tip is to check the buildings and supply bins and head to a better location.

MARKET

This indoor market is a cool location and can be used to find some good loot, but it can also be a trap. There's lots of ways into it and it can be attractive for anyone looking to steal from the destroyed storefronts. Be ready for close-range battles inside and medium-range ones when you leave.

EPIC
MOMENTS

Play *Apex* for any amount of time and you'll likely come back with an epic story of your own. The matches seem perfect for these little stories that you'll come back to tell your friends. Here are some of ours – try to recreate them or make your own!

ZIPLINE TO DEATH

Pathfinder's zipline is useful for getting your team around Kings Canyon, but it also can be used by enemies. One way to use that to your advantage is to create a zipline so that it sends people shooting off cliffs to their deaths. Hilarious players have baited enemy squads towards a dangerous zipline, one they know they need to jump off early because it wasn't safe. Their enemies followed and plunged to their deaths.

FISTICUFFS

Look around online and you can find multiple videos showing battles that came down to a single fist-fight. When there are only two players left, punching in the air will signify to the other player that you want to handle things like true warriors. Then let those fists fly!

CHAPPIE?!?

The director of *Chappie* (Neill Blomkamp) stated on Twitter that everyone was asking him about getting a Chappie skin for Pathfinder into the game and that he's down for it. The founder of Respawn replied to him stating, "I am also down." We haven't seen the skin just yet, but we can hope!

GRANDPA GAMER

Twitch streamer GrndPaGaming is a retired Navy Diver who streamed an epic game where he showed that he's better than players half his age. With his entire squad downed, he quickly eliminated an enemy player and then no-scoped the last two players in the squad, one after the other!

TRAPPING YOUR ENEMY

Bunker is a favourite location for Caustic, who can actually seal doors using his gas traps. Players who know better can shoot them and get in or out, but players have loved using this area to trap unsuspecting players. A cleverly-timed portal followed by a gas-laden room has taken out more than one squad.

HILARIOUS GLITCHES

Any game as popular as *Apex Legends* is bound to run into funny glitches. Some broke the game, while some have proven useful! Respawn's hard-working team quickly patches out these issues as they come up, but not before we've all had a good laugh.

PORTAL TO NOWHERE

Players found that if you opened one of Wraith's portals in a doorway and then closed the door, anyone going through the other portal would be instantly killed when they tried to inhabit door-occupied space. Talk about a doorstop.

STICKY SHIELDS

Some genius realised that Gibraltar's shields are sticky and then players went wild. If the person playing Gibraltar holds out his shield, Caustic can throw his gas tanks onto it and they will stick. This lead to Gibraltars walking around with multiple gas tanks sticking out – a portable gas weapon! This bug also allowed Octane's jump pads to stick, allowing for awesome mobile jump pads!

» BIRD IN FLIGHT «

HERE'S SOMETHING TO TRY THE NEXT TIME YOU JUMP. HOW FAR CAN YOU FLY? IT'S EASY TO ZOOM STRAIGHT DOWN TO THE GROUND, BUT HOW FAR ACROSS THE MAP CAN YOU GLIDE? FINDING THOSE REMOTE SPOTS ALLOW YOU TO GET A FEW MINUTES PEACE BEFORE COMBAT STARTS!

ETERNAL FLIGHT

An early glitch saw players figuring out a way to launch players back up into the stratosphere while gliding down to a match. Over and over you would be able to jump back up into the sky, staying out of the battle for as long as you wanted.

RAPID-FIRE PEACEKEEPER

This one was hard to perform, but players found that by performing a series of button presses it was possible to fire all of a Peacekeeper's shots like it was an automatic shotgun. In order to do so you had to fire the Peacekeeper, switch to a secondary weapon and then switch back. This would skip the weapon's long reload animation and allow you to fire over and over as long as you didn't jumble up the buttons. Considering the amount of damage the gun can do, it made it truly OP and was patched out after being discovered.

UBERGLIDE

This jump tower glitch made it possible to glide far across the map! The only way to do this was to keep aiming straight up into the sky while facing the direction you wanted to go. That would give you an absolutely massive boost that would keep happening every time you got near the ground!

THE BEST SKINS

While you can play the game just fine without spending money, Respawn is making sure that there are plenty of different Legend skins available for you. This lets you customise your favourite character and stand out from the crowd. They can be found in Apex Packs from levelling up or simply purchased, although some of the coolest ones were only available in limited events.

PATHFINDER
OMEGA POINT

A Twitch-only exclusive, this purple and silver skin makes Pathfinder really stand out. Maybe this 'bot will look cool enough to get a high five?

BLOODHOUND
THE PLAGUE DOCTOR

Pretend you're treating the bubonic plague with this not-at-all-terrifying doctor's outfit! It doesn't seem like it would help a tracker, but when you look this scary, who's complaining?

CAUSTIC
BLACKHEART

Throw away Caustic's clinical look for one that looks geared for war. Those furs and spiked boots make him look ready for the cold but really it's his cold, cold heart you'll have to worry about!

BANGALORE
OFFICER WILLIAMS

Bangalore knows more than anyone about weapons, so she'd be an incredible police officer. With this armour (and those shades!) you definitely will be obeying everything she says.

WRAITH
NIGHT TERROR

This was an exclusive to anyone who bought the Wild Frontier Battle Pass and was well worth the money. Wraith looks absolutely primal here.

GIBRALTAR
DARK SIDE

Gibraltar is usually a pretty happy guy, even in battle, so it's curious to see him embrace the dark side. You do not want to run into this mountain of a man.

OCTANE
EL DIABLO

Dios mio! Octane's devil get-up is probably the coolest skin of the bunch. He almost looks like a new Legend!

MIRAGE
TIE-DYE

The most flamboyant Legend deserves the most flamboyant skin. For someone who wants to be the centre of attention, there's nothing better than tie-dye.

LIFELINE
VITAL SIGNS

This outfit looks like someone from the 1980s' view of futuristic clothing. The Red Cross-style look shows exactly what she's there for too.

EASTER EGGS & SECRETS

Respawn Entertainment loves to fill their games full of secrets for their long-time fans, as well as adding little references to pop culture and their fanbase. Keep an eye out during matches, you never know what you're going to find!

FOR THE BIRDS

Fan of *Overwatch*? There's a nod to Bastion in *Apex Legends* in Pathfinder's pose called 'For The Birds'.
Bastion is a robot in *Overwatch* who loves nature and has a little bird friend. Pathfinder is a robot skilled at a human deathsport as well, but he doesn't exactly have the same relationship with nature.

[Arzamar]

5

KILLS

0

NO DATA

NO DATA

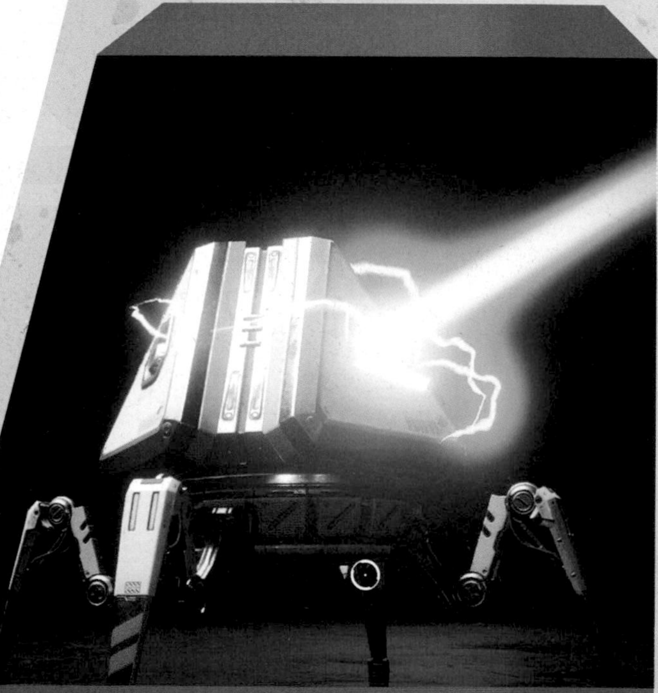

LOOT TICKS

You might see these little robots standing around, but more likely you'll hear them first. If you ever hear strange whirrs and clicks, look around for a Loot Tick. They look like Apex Packs with legs and always hold great loot. You can smash them open with a melee attack or by shooting them. They'll drop three random pieces of loot. The colour of the loot tick shows the quality of items inside it – run straight to them and get that loot!

HEIRLOOM SETS

Everyone loves loot, but what you might not know is that there's one piece of loot that's harder to find than any other. That's the Heirloom Set, which is so rare that the game only shipped with one for Wraith!

Wraith's Heirloom Set contains an exclusive Banner Pose, Melee Weapon Skin and Intro Quip. The best part by far is the melee weapon skin, because it allows you to hold a knife. Wraith doesn't do any more melee damage with that knife than anyone else that's unarmed, but it sure looks cool.

The only problem is finding this set! Open an Apex Pack and you'll have lower than a 1% chance of getting one of these. There's no other way to get one, since you can't craft it with materials or buy it in the store. You just have to be lucky.

You are guaranteed to get one after opening 500 packs, but considering each pack costs around £1, that's a really pricey way to go about getting one. Maybe you'll just be super lucky one day?

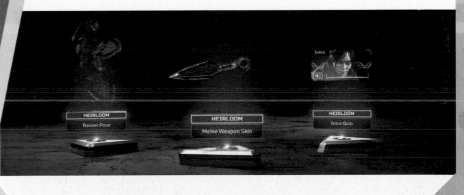

NESSIE

Respawn loves the Loch Ness Monster. In both *Titanfall* and *Titanfall 2* there was a hidden plush of 'Nessie' that could be found and *Apex Legends* has them too! We found this one tucked away in the Training Level of the game – can you find the rest?

There are 10 hidden in Kings Canyon and if you manage to find them all in order, you might just unlock a big surprise ...

FLYERS

You'll notice little dragons perched around the map called Flyers. They're loud, so they're hard to miss. But have you tried shooting them? If you do, you'll discover a surprise – they're holding onto death boxes of people on your friends list! The purple boxes usually have some good loot in them, so make sure to fire on the flyers whenever you can do it safely. Just try not to think too hard about what happened to your friends ...

HOW MANY MAP LOCATIONS CAN YOU FIND?

B	L	N	Q	O	U	U	V	E	O	B	F	X	T	R
S	U	G	A	I	R	B	A	S	E	F	Z	N	S	O
A	T	H	U	N	D	E	R	D	O	M	E	L	T	S
T	R	M	S	H	G	N	P	N	S	M	U	B	E	L
O	H	T	A	Z	Z	S	U	D	T	M	Z	R	K	U
Q	Q	E	I	D	B	R	N	A	L	E	O	I	R	P
R	Y	W	P	L	O	A	E	A	X	R	S	D	A	E
M	Y	S	A	I	L	R	K	H	H	E	K	G	M	R
P	R	W	K	T	T	E	D	Z	Q	L	U	E	T	M
S	U	N	E	R	S	S	R	Y	W	A	L	S	D	H
J	C	W	E	C	S	M	Y	Y	H	Y	L	I	X	M
P	O	T	S	E	D	A	C	S	A	C	T	U	H	X
R	A	R	E	K	N	U	B	U	P	L	O	D	N	G
W	B	S	W	A	M	P	S	Q	Z	E	W	Q	A	T
I	X	I	T	X	T	H	W	Z	O	W	N	D	E	C

AIRBASE
ARTILLERY
BRIDGES
BUNKER
CASCADES
HYDRODAM

MARKET
RELAY
REPULSOR
RUNOFF
SKULLTOWN

SLUM LAKES
SWAMPS
THE PIT
THUNDERDOME
WATER TREATMENT
WETLANDS

ANSWERS ON PAGE 68

HOW WELL DO YOU KNOW YOUR LEGENDS?

To become a Champion in you need to know what you're up against. You can choose your main and only play as one Legend, sure, but you'll still need to know everyone's abilities so you're ready for what's coming. Draw a line from the Legend to their tactical ability!

PSYCHE OUT

INTO THE VOID

NOX GAS TRAP

SMOKE LAUNCHER

EYE OF THE ALLFATHER

DOME OF PROTECTION

PERIMETER SECURITY

GRAPPLING HOOK

STIM

D.O.C. HEAL DRONE

0 CORRECT
Maybe you should try playing the game first?

1-4 CORRECT
You need to branch out and try new characters!

5-9 CORRECT
You know your way around the roster!

10 CORRECT
You're a LEGEND, and ready for anything that comes next!

Answers: Caustic - Nox Gas Trap, Gibraltar - Dome of Protection, Wattson - Perimeter Security, Bangalore - Smoke Launcher, Mirage - Psyche Out, Octane - Stim, Wraith - Into the Void, Bloodhound - Eye of the Allfather, Lifeline - D.O.C. Heal Drone, Pathfinder - Grappling Hook

CHEATS DON'T DO IT

Look, it happens to all of us. You have a bad game. You're frustrated, you keep getting killed right away and feel like everyone is playing better than you. You also know that there's cheating software that would allow you to get all the kills and maybe finally become a Champion!

There's a lot of dodgy software out there that can give you a leg up. There are aimbots that make it so that you're a crack shot – the software will give the player automatic headshots without even having to aim, or even allow someone to shoot through walls. There are also speed hacks that increase a player's movement speed and fire-rate to ridiculous levels, making them hard to hit and easier for them to stay in the ring. There's even X-Ray vision that allows people to see through obstacles.

They sound great, right? Trust us – it's not worth it. Not only is cheating a really weak move, it will likely lead to you getting banned from ever playing the game again.

Respawn Entertainment has banned hundreds of thousands of players who cheated in the game. In May 2019 they announced that they're "attacking this from every angle", banning 770K cheaters in total. They identify who you are by your HWID (Hardware ID), which means that when they ban you, you will never be able to use that computer to play *Apex Legends* ever again. The only way you could play is by getting a brand-new computer!

That sounds harsh, but only by wielding the ban hammer in such a brutal way can they prove that cheaters never win. Sure, you might rack up a few wins if you cheat – but you don't want to risk it. Play fair and win like a true Champion!

» BEST TEAM KILL RECORD

A SQUAD OF THREE PLAYERS (NOOOK, GNASKE_LONE_TTV, AND YA_EM_DETEI_ LOL) GOT 46 KILLS IN A SINGLE MATCH!

UPCOMING SEASONS

While Respawn Entertainment likes to keep things close to their chest as far as the future of *Apex Legends*, they do love listening to the community and have promised to keep making new content as long as people keep playing!

BATTLE PASS MASTER QUIZ

Can you unlock all 100 ranks in a season? There's an exclusive Legendary weapon skin for you if you do!

WEAPONS

Each season of the game will feature at least one new weapon. There are plenty more that they could grab from *Titanfall*, but we expect them to make brand-new ones that surprise us all. Expect all kinds of new skins for existing weapons to appear in the store as well!

» BAMBOOZLE « THE WORLD!

HOW WELL CAN YOU MIMIC A HOLOGRAPH? MIRAGE PLAYERS LIKE TO STAND OUT IN THE OPEN OR RUN INTO WALLS, ALL TO FOOL PLAYERS INTO THINKING THEY'RE REALLY A DECOY!

Updates will be broken up into 'Seasons', just like *Fortnite*. Every three months or so a new season will begin, each of which will have a new Battle Pass with unique challenges, a new Legend to unlock, new weapons and new loot.

"Season 1 is just the first version on a long road of improvements, updates and tweaks," says Respawn.

TITANS

Anyone who has played *Titanfall* knows how incredible it is to call in a massive mech, jump in and run around raining destruction. These Titans are a key part of the game and so this is a much-requested feature for *Apex Legends*, but no one knows how it could work. Would these metal monstrosities overwhelm squads? How could they make them fair?

FLYERS

Right before the launch of Season 2, dragon-like Flyers appeared in the skies above Kings Canyon. They swoop in holding loot boxes and will drop them if shot. But this is just the beginning – there are a lot of creatures in the *Apex Legends* universe. Besides the giant monsters walking around in the background, the developers have teased a giant eye belonging to a massive beast to fight, as well as possible flying game modes in concept art.

We do know that Respawn prototyped Titans in the game for nine months. While that doesn't mean that it will definitely happen in the future, it does mean that if they do decide to put them in, they've already done the legwork.

LEAKED CHARACTERS!

Players have loved data-mining *Apex Legends* files – sifting through patches and updates to reveal the names of new files – and trying to figure out what their names mean for what's coming next.

Because of these efforts we knew about new Legends like Octane and Wattson months before they were even announced and there are even more on the way! Here are some names and abilities that have been found. Will they all definitely appear one day? Well, none of this has been confirmed by Respawn Entertainment yet, but we do know there are new Legends on the way, so don't be surprised to see some of them very soon!

BLACKOUT

There are no details about this character yet, but from the name maybe it's someone that messes with other player's vision in some way?

HUSARIA

Hussars were elite Polish cavalry between the 16th and 18th centuries. While it's doubtful this character will have a mount of some kind, leaked concept art looks like they have some sort of robot arm on their back.

CRYPTO

This Legend appears to be wearing a sword, and there's a cooldown called 'Swordblock' in the files. Could they be able to deflect bullets with their sword? If it is, it could be similar to the Titan 'Ronin', a giant mech that used swordblock to defend itself.

JERICHO

Wearing a hoodie like an *Assassin's Creed* character, leaked art of Jericho shows someone strapped with a weapon, indicating a potential offensive Legend.

ROSIE

The Riveter? An engineering background could indicate a support or defensive character.

PROPHET

Looks like Prophet might be able to tell the future. Data miners have found that Prophet has an ability called 'Precog', which is a HUD element. Maybe an ability similar to Wraith's, or something that allows you to see incoming drop pods?

RAMPART

This looks to be a defensive Legend and the name agrees with that. He's rumoured to have some sort of riot shield, perhaps similar to Gibraltar's.

NOMAD

Early images show a skull-clad Legend that's completely covered up. We know that Bloodhound hides their identity, so maybe this is another recon character.

SKUNNER

An image of Skunner shows a potential support class character wearing a huge backpack of some kind. What's inside it is anyone's guess right now ...

GLOSSARY

CHAMPION
The winner of the match, the star of the Apex Games.

COOLDOWN
How long it takes for you to be able to use an ability again. The best ones have longer cooldowns!

DEATH BOX
These are dropped after a player is eliminated from the game. It's got all their loot in it!

DPS
Damage Per Second. How much damage you can do with a weapon.

ELIMINATED
When you bleed out or are killed after being knocked down. You're out, but you can still be respawned!

FULLY KITTED
A weapon equipped with every possible attachment.

HIPSHOT
Firing without aiming down the sights. It's not as accurate, but it's faster.

HP
Hit Points. Your health.

JUMPMASTER
The player who decides where their squad lands. An essential role.

KNOCKED DOWN
When your HP hits 0 you'll fall to the ground. A friend can still revive you, if you're lucky.

LEGEND
The characters in *Apex Legends*. Each one is unique!

RATE OF FIRE/FIRE-RATE
How fast a weapon fires. Higher rates of fire mean more damage.

THE RING
Apex's version of The Storm. It's ever-shrinking and always dangerous.

NO-SCOPE
Same as firing from the hip, but with a sniper rifle. These are difficult shots to pull off!

OP
Overpowered. Some weapons are OP and have to be patched so that the game is fair.

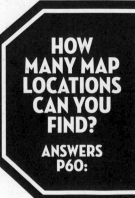

HOW MANY MAP LOCATIONS CAN YOU FIND?

ANSWERS P60:

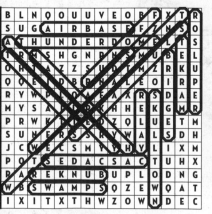

ONLINE SAFETY

Apex Legends features a more realistic visual style compared to similar games and is rated as suitable for players 16 years of age and over by PEGI. We've put together some simple rules to help you stay safe and keep the internet an awesome place to spend time.

GENERAL ONLINE SAFETY

» Never give out your real name – don't use it as your username.
» Never give out any of your personal details.
» Never tell anybody your password.
» Take regular breaks from playing.
» Always report any incidence of cheating or harassment.

ONLINE CHAT

In *Apex Legends*, there is live, unmoderated voice chat between users. You can navigate to the Settings section in the lobby, select the Audio tab and reduce the Voice Chat Volume down to 0 to turn off any voice chat from any player. You can still communicate with the ping system.

If you would like to keep voice chat on, but don't want to hear from certain individuals, you can do that too. Open your inventory during a match and scroll to the Squad tab. Find the player that you want to mute and select the speaker icon beneath their image.

SOCIAL MEDIA SCAMS

There are many accounts on social media sites like Facebook and Twitter that claim to give away free Apex Coins and other currencies, which will be transferred to their account. Be sceptical – it's important to check the authenticity of these accounts and offers before giving away personal information.

IN-GAME PURCHASES

Apex Legends does offer the ability to make in-game purchases such as the Battle Pass and cosmetic skins, but they're not required to play the game. They also don't improve a player's performance.

SOUND

Apex Legends is a game where sound is crucial. Players will often wear headphones, meaning parents won't be able to hear what is being said by strangers. Set up your console or computer to have sound coming from the TV as well as the headset so you can hear what other players are saying to your child.

PARENTAL CONTROLS

Apex Legends doesn't have any parental controls due to its PEGI 16 rating. If your suitably-aged child is playing the game, exercise caution and check in regularly to make sure you know how, and with whom, they're playing.

SCREEN TIME

Taking regular breaks is important. Set play sessions by using a timer. However, *Apex Legends* games can last up to 30 minutes and if your child finishes playing in the middle of a round, they'll leave their teammates a person short and lose any points they've earned. It's advisable to give advanced warning for stopping play.